Pathfinder 31

Teaching learners how to learn:
strategy training in the ML classroom

⌣ *NLIV* 2000

Dave

The *Pathfinder* Series

Active learning — listening and reading

Reading for pleasure in a foreign language (PF2)
Ann Swarbrick
ISBN 0 948003 98 7

Developing skills for independent reading (PF22)
Iain Mitchell & Ann Swarbrick
ISBN 1 874016 34 8

Creative use of texts (PF21)
Bernard Kavanagh & Lynne Upton
ISBN 1 874016 28 3

Listening in a foreign language (PF26)
A skill we take for granted?
Karen Turner
ISBN 1 874016 44 5

Supporting learners and learning

Teaching learners how to learn
Strategy training in the ML classroom (PF31)
Vee Harris
ISBN 1 874016 83 6

Making effective use of the dictionary (PF28)
Gwen Berwick and Phil Horsfall
ISBN 1 874016 60 7

Nightshift (PF20)
Ideas and strategies for homework
David Buckland & Mike Short
ISBN 1 874016 19 4

Grammar matters (PF17)
Susan Halliwell
ISBN 1 874016 12 7

Planning and organising teaching

Assessment and planning in the MFL department (PF29)
Harmer Parr
ISBN 1 874016 71 2

Departmental planning and schemes of work (PF11)
Clive Hurren
ISBN 1 874016 10 0

Fair enough? (PF14)
Equal opportunities and modern languages
Vee Harris
ISBN 1 874016 03 8

Making the case for languages (PF8)
Alan Moys & Richard Townsend
ISBN 0 948003 79 0

Bridging the gap (PF7)
GCSE to 'A' level
John Thorogood & Lid King
ISBN 0 948003 89 8

Improve your image (PF15)
The effective use of the OHP
Daniel Tierney & Fay Humphreys
ISBN 1 874016 04 6

Teaching/learning in the target language

On target (PF5)
Teaching in the target language
Susan Halliwell & Barry Jones
ISBN 0 948003 54 5

Keeping on target (PF23)
Bernardette Holmes
ISBN 1 874016 35 5

Motivating all learners

Yes — but will they behave? (PF4)
Managing the interactive classroom
Susan Halliwell
ISBN 0 948003 44 8

Not bothered? (PF16)
Motivating reluctant language learners in Key Stage 4
Jenifer Alison
ISBN 1 874016 06 2

Communication re-activated (PF6)
Teaching pupils with learning difficulties
Bernardette Holmes
ISBN 0 948003 59 6

Differentiation (PF18)
Taking the initiative
Anne Convery & Do Coyle
ISBN 1 874016 18 6

Cultural awareness

Crossing frontiers (PF30)
The school study visit abroad
David Snow & Michael Byram
ISBN 1 874016 84 4

Languages home and away (PF9)
Alison Taylor
ISBN 0 948003 84 7

Exploring otherness (PF24)
An approach to cultural awareness
Barry Jones
ISBN 1 874016 42 9

Broadening the learning experience

New contexts for modern language learning (PF27)
Cross-curricular approaches
Kim Brown & Margot Brown
ISBN 1 874016 50 X

With a song in my scheme of work (PF25)
Steven Fawkes
ISBN 1 874016 45 3

Drama in the languages classroom (PF19)
Judith Hamilton & Anne McLeod
ISBN 1 874016 07 0

Being Creative (PF10)
Barry Jones
ISBN 0 948003 99 5

All Pathfinders are available through good book suppliers or direct from **Grantham Book Services,** Isaac Newton Way, Alma Park Industrial Estate, Grantham, Lincs NG31 9SD.
Fax orders to: 01476 541 061. Credit card orders: 01476 541 080

Pathfinder 31

A CILT series for language teachers

Teaching learners how to learn

Strategy training in the ML classroom

Vee Harris

CiLT

Centre for Information
on Language Teaching and Research

The views expressed in this publication are the author's and do not necessarily represent those of CILT.

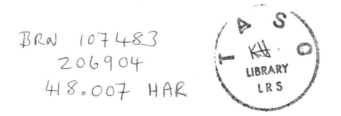

First published 1997
Copyright © 1997 Centre for Information on Language Teaching and Research
ISBN 1 874016 83 6

A catalogue record for this book is available from the British Library
Printed in Great Britain by Oakdale Printing Co Ltd

Published by the Centre for Information on Language Teaching and Research,
20 Bedfordbury, Covent Garden, London WC2N 4LB

CILT Publications are available from: Grantham Book Services, Isaac Newton Way,
Alma Park Industrial Estate, Grantham, Lincs NG31 8SD. Tel: 01476 541 080.
Fax: 01476 541 061. Book trade representation (UK and Ireland): Broadcast Book
Services, 24 De Montfort Road, London SW16 1LZ. Tel: 0181 677 5129.

Contents

Page

Introduction   1

1 What are learning strategies?   4

2 Strategies under the microscope   6
Section 1   6
Section 2   9

3 Why teach learning strategies?   11

4 How to teach learning strategies: the strategy training cycle   13
The strategy training cycle   13
  1 Awareness raising   13
  2 Modelling   14
  3 Action planning/goal setting   14
  4 Extensive practice   15
  5 Fading out the reminders   15

5 The strategy training cycle in action   16
Teaching memorisation strategies   16
Teaching reading strategies   18
Teaching pupils to check their work   22

6 There's no time!   25
Building the cycle in the scheme of work   25
What about the target language?   28

7 Taking it further   29

References   32

Acknowledgements

This book would not have been possible without the hard work, energy and initiative of the following teachers and advisory teachers who have completed the CILT/Goldsmiths MA module:

- Angelina Adams
- Marian Carty
- Pamela Dewey
- Jacqueline Footman
- Fiona Lunsky

The module brings together teachers from different parts of the country to explore ways of developing pupil independence and of teaching learner strategies. Many of the ideas presented here stem from their experiences in translating theoretical ideas into practical activities for the classroom across a range of schools, age and attainment groups.

I am particularly indebted to Marian Carty who helped move my thinking forward when we worked together to develop ideas and materials for a joint presentation on 'Learner Strategies' at a Scottish CILT conference in February 1996.

A key figure in the MA course is Dr Michael Grenfell of Southampton University who shares the planning and teaching with me. In addition to this work, however, the book owes much to the many discussions we have had in which new ideas have been generated, rejected or developed. He has been a patient guide through the realms of the complex research literature and an encouraging and supportive colleague.

I am also very grateful to Ann Swarbrick (the Open University) who first showed me the Dutch poem, to Diane Place (St Andrews School, Croydon) for sharing with me her work on 'Boys' underachievement' and to the students on the PGCE Modern Languages course at Goldsmiths College who took up the ideas and implemented them with such enthusiasm and imagination in their classrooms.

Finally, I want to thank my daughter, Sophie, for providing many of the illustrations.

Introduction

The current concern to 'raise achievement' in all areas of the curriculum may leave modern language teachers feeling that they should be drawing yet more colourful flashcards, devising further sets of differentiated worksheets or creating a choice of even more imaginative creative outcomes. An alternative approach is to focus on enabling the pupils themselves to become more effective learners in order that the responsibility for their progress may be shared between the teacher and the pupils. This book is about giving pupils the tools or strategies to learn more effectively.

To get a sense of what these strategies are, it may be helpful to start by translating as much as you can of the following Dutch text:

Een appel is rood,
de zon is geel,
de hemel is blauw,
een blad is groen,
een wolk is wit . . .
en de aarde is bruin.

En zou je nu kunnen
antwoorden
op de vraag . . .

Given that modern language teachers are usually interested in the way any new language operates, it is likely that you managed to work out the meaning of most of the poem, although the last sentence may have caused some difficulties. A clue is provided on the next page of the text where it says 'what colour is love?'. The full translation is provided on p31.

In order to gain some insight into the strategies that you, as a successful linguist, use, it is worth reflecting on exactly what you did that allowed you to work out the meaning of a poem in a completely unfamiliar language.

It is likely that the strategies you used included a combination of some of the following:

1 recognising the type of text (in this case, a poem in a child's book) and therefore having some expectations of what it might be about, its overall structure, etc;
2 looking for cognates (words that look or sound familiar through knowledge of English, German, Spanish, etc);
3 using common sense and knowledge of the world (apples are not blue!);
4 using the pattern of the sentences to make sensible guesses ('a something is + colour');
5 saying the text out loud;
6 using the pictures (although not everyone notices the little drawings behind the children).

We should perhaps add to the list something along the lines of 'using knowledge of grammar', since that is probably essential to unpack the more complex final sentence.

These kinds of strategies are obviously very helpful in enabling us to tackle a new language, so why not let pupils in on the secret and make our own knowledge explicit? After all, strategies were one of the things that allowed us, the language teachers, to become so good at learning languages when we were pupils in the classroom. Most of us used a wide range of tools or tactics to help us learn, without even consciously thinking about them. It may be, however, that many of our pupils are not aware of such strategies and that, if we deliberately set out to teach them, they too might become more successful learners.

If you want to find out what other strategies successful language learners have in their repertoire, use yourself as an example before reading the next section. What did you do to learn either your first foreign language or your second? For example:

• How did you memorise vocabulary?
• How did you memorise grammar rules?

- How did you go about checking and redrafting your written work?
- What did you do when you had something to say but did not know the precise word?
- What did you do when listening to a radio programme and there was something you did not immediately understand?

You may want to compare your strategies to those that have been identified in the research literature. A summary of some of the most common ones can be found in Chapter 2. Although some of the strategies listed may not be applicable to younger learners, they do provide some insight into the overall mental processes used by successful language learners.

1   What are learning strategies?

Recent years have been marked by an increasing interest in learner autonomy (Dickinson, 1987; Holec, 1988; Little, 1991). The CILT publication *Letting go — taking hold* (Page (ed), 1992) describes a range of ways in which teachers have set about handing over to pupils responsibility for their own learning. As Nunan (1995) points out, however:

> *It is a mistake to assume that learners come into the language classroom with a natural ability to make choices about what and how to learn.*

This first became evident to me when I started to work with a group of London teachers to explore how to take the initial steps away from a teacher-centred classroom. We gradually began to be aware of a range of problems (Grenfell and Harris, 1993). Many of the pupils did not know how to use a dictionary. They were reduced to panic when faced with reading authentic material without the teacher's support, and some of them lacked the basic social skills to support each other in group work. It seemed that for autonomy to work, it was not enough to organise the classroom in such a way that a range of resources and activities were on offer. Pupils had to be taught the skills and strategies they needed to tackle things on their own. Only in that way could they be expected to make the most of the opportunities offered them.

Before considering how to teach the strategies, we may want to be clearer about what these strategies are and if some are more 'teachable' than others. There is a bewildering array of descriptions of strategies in the research literature. Unfortunately a great deal of the research has been carried out on learners of English living in America, often studying at university level. We are only just beginning to explore the strategies used by pupils in British secondary schools to find out which are similar and which are different.

One popular distinction in the literature differentiates between Communication Strategies and Learning Strategies. Broadly speaking, **Communication Strategies** are a set of 'coping' tactics for keeping the communication channel open when the learners' linguistic repertoire is not quite wide enough either to understand what has just been said or to express what they want to say next. These strategies include circumlocution, making up words, asking for help, and 'stalling strategies' such as *'bof, ben, je ne sais pas moi'* that we use to give ourselves time to think.

CiLT

Learning Strategies on the other hand are more to do with how we go about our learning. O'Malley and Chamot (1990) draw a distinction here between 'metacognitive' and 'cognitive' strategies. The first group relates to the more global strategies involved in planning, monitoring and then evaluating learning; deciding for example how to tackle a particular task and then evaluating how successfully we have done it. The second group refers to strategies used for specific language tasks involving direct manipulation of the language, whether it is basic 'study skills' like memorisation strategies, or more complex ones like applying grammar rules. A third group they identified were 'social and affective' strategies through which the learner may seek help from others or control emotional responses, such as level of anxiety.

It appears that it is more fruitful to teach Learning Strategies than Communication Strategies (Bialystock, 1990). This is because it is hard to bring spontaneous speech under conscious control, to think not only about what you want to say next but also which strategy to use to get round any problems encountered. The personality of the learner may also be a factor; the will to communicate at all costs is not easy to instill in all our pupils! That said, we can at least set about teaching pupils some of the simpler Communication Strategies. Expressions like *'cómo se dice pencil en español'* and *'no comprendo'* should be taught in as systematic a way as we would teach the language of any other new topic. We can also encourage pupils to use them on a regular basis so that they interrupt and interact with our input, rather than just letting the target language flow over them. Some teachers also hang cards with 'stalling strategies' written on them from the ceiling, so that when pupils get stuck, they can glance heavenwards for help!

In the long term it may be that we have to recognise that some of the more complex Communication Strategies will develop only once Learning Strategies have allowed pupils sufficient access to the language. Circumlocution, for example, is hard to achieve if your linguistic repertoire is very limited, although one pupil I taught did manage to produce *'maisons des poissons'* to convey 'shells'. Drama situations, where props and cue cards are used deliberately to provoke tension, conflict or misunderstanding are also more likely to stimulate the development of Communication Strategies than safe, predictable and rehearsed role plays. Pupils need to understand, however, that what is required is not accuracy or even fluency, but the ability to find any means possible as a way round a particular communication problem. Making the criteria explicit in this way will not only encourage them to 'take risks' in the target language, but also offers them some insight into the different levels or areas involved in operating in a new language.

2   Strategies under the microscope

There is considerable debate in the research literature regarding:

- what constitutes a strategy. Are study skills strategies, for example?
- what constitutes evidence of a strategy being used. After all, how can we know what is going on in a pupil's head as they read through a text or perform a role play?
- how strategies can best be described and classified. Should they be classified according to the four skills or to the division between Learning and Communication Strategies or, as O'Malley and Chamot do, according to the distinction between 'metacognitive', 'cognitive' and 'affective' strategies?

However interesting the questions are on a theoretical level, on a practical level we need some form of strategy checklist to provide a starting point for embarking on teaching them. There's little point in teaching strategies that pupils are already using. The following lists are an attempt to summarise in as clear a way as possible ideas drawn from a wide range of sources; from the research literature, from studies Dr Grenfell and I have undertaken as well as ideas from teachers on the CILT/Goldsmiths MA Module. They have been classified, for ease of reference, under broad skill areas; the first section covers the strategies involved in each of the four skills. The second section covers more general strategies such as study skills, planning work, etc. Inevitably, much of the complex research has been simplified.

The summary could be used as a checklist in a number of ways:

- adding strategies you yourself used as a learner;
- adding strategies you have noticed your pupils using;
- ticking strategies your pupils already use;
- crossing strategies they do not use but you would like them to;
- indicating the year group most appropriate for teaching that particular strategy.

SECTION 1

There is clearly considerable overlap between the strategies involved in the 'receptive' skills of reading and listening. For both skill areas, the order in which the strategies are listed indicates a broad continuum starting from those that might be associated with 'top-down' processing (global comprehension of the meaning of text as a whole) to those indicative of a 'bottom-up' approach (word-for-word translation, 'decoding').

CiLT

LISTENING

1 Recognising the type of listening text; conversation/advert/news programme?

2 Recognising the topic; going for gist.

3 Predicting on the basis of knowledge of the world; what is likely/unlikely in this situation?

4 Using the tone of speakers' voices for clues (and facial gestures in the case of video).

5 Picking out cognates.

6 Identifying unfamiliar phrases and playing the relevant section of the tape over and over again.

7 Holding the unfamiliar sounds in your head; saying them over and over.

8 Trying to break down the stream of sound into individual words.

9 Trying to write the sounds down and to relate them to written words previously learned.

10 Listening out for clues from the tense, word order, etc.

11

12

READING

1 Recognising the type of text; poem, newspaper article, brochure?

2 Examining pictures, the title, etc for clues.

3 Going for gist, skipping inessential words.

4 Saying the text outloud and identifying 'chunk boundaries'; how a sentence breaks down and which parts of it to work on at one time.

5 Using knowledge of the world to make sensible guesses.

6 Picking out cognates.

7 Substituting English words, e.g. 'she something on his head'.

8 Analysing unknown words, breaking a word/phrase down and associating parts of it to familiar words, e.g. 'hochgewachsen'.

9 Identifying the grammatical category of words.

10 Using punctuation for clues; question marks, capital letters, etc.

11

12

SPEAKING

There is a wide range of strategies involved in producing speech, including 'Making the most of what you have got', 'Using set phrases', 'Picking up and using a word/phrase you have just heard the native speaker say', etc. Here we only list those generally accepted as Communication Strategies.

1 Keeping it simple; avoiding topics or concepts which pose particular problems.
2 Changing the way you were going to say something so that you can use an easier expression.
3 Approximation; using a word which has roughly the same meaning.
4 Circumlocution; describing something, what it does/looks like, to explain the meaning.
5 Using 'all purpose words', e.g. *le truc*.
6 Making up a word.
7 Saying an English word but with a French/German accent.
8 Using mime, gesture, facial expression.
9 Asking for help; 'how do you say . . ?'
10 Using 'fillers' or 'stalling' strategies, e.g. *'Bof', 'Eh bien'* to give yourself time to think.
11
12

Many of the above strategies can also be used in writing, e.g. keeping it simple, circumlocution, approximation and 'all-purpose words'.

WRITING

1 Sorting out what the task requires and some ideas of what you want to say; working out the order in which you will express the ideas.
2 Making the most of what you have got.
3 Adding ideas as you start to write.
4 Recalling relevant previously learned words/phrases.
5 Using set expressions, stock phrases, possibly replacing one or two words in a set phrase.
6 Using clear markers, e.g. 'firstly', 'on the other hand'.
7 'Making it fancy'; using clause links, e.g. *'que, dont'*.
8 Trying out grammatical rules in a new context.
9 Using the dictionary, reference books, looking for synonyms.
10 Drafting and redrafting.
11
12

CiLT

Teaching specific strategies for specific skills is of little value unless pupils reach the point where they can decide for themselves which strategies are appropriate for a particular task, where they can function independently. The strategies in this second section, particularly the metacognitive strategies of **monitoring** and **planning** learning, are of critical significance since they remind us of the inextricable link between strategy training and autonomy and that strategy training cannot be considered as a bolt-on addition to a wholly teacher-centred classroom. Collaborative project-based work is essential to offer pupils opportunities to monitor and direct their own learning, to develop the strategies they personally need, and to work together so that they can 'borrow' each other's approach to the task in hand. As Little (1997) suggests:

> *If the pursuit of learner autonomy requires that we focus explicitly on the strategic component of language learning and language use, the reverse should also be the case: focus on strategies should lead us to learner autonomy.*

Monitoring your own progress becomes part and parcel of **planning** what you need to do next and how to go about it.

MONITORING

A   Monitoring learning
1   Strategy monitoring: tracking how well a strategy is working
2   Self-assessment:
  • identifying what has been successfully grasped and what needs further work;
  • judging one's ability to perform a task;
  • judging one's overall execution of the task. This will entail:

B   Monitoring language use
This is obviously easier in written work (where the learner has time to reflect and correct) than in spontaneous speech.
1   Auditory monitoring: 'does it sound right?'
2   Visual monitoring: 'does it look right?'
3   Grammatical monitoring: 'is that the right tense, adjectival agreement?', etc.
4   Style monitoring, e.g. 'is that the right tone for a formal letter?'
5
6
'Comprehension monitoring' ('does that really make sense?') is important for both reading and listening.

PLANNING

1 Organisational planning; deciding how to handle a task, e.g. devising a plan for the parts, sequence, main ideas to be used in a written task.

2 Selective attention; deciding what to concentrate on, e.g. the gist in a listening exercise or verb endings in redrafting work. Realising that your concentration is slipping when listening to a tape.

3 Problem identification; identifying what it is that is holding you up, e.g. 'We can't write this letter because we don't know how to start it off by saying 'Thank you for your Christmas present'.

4 Plan monitoring, e.g. 'I thought I could do this by just reading it through for gist but do I need to go back now and read each sentence through more slowly and look out for some cognates?'

5 Self-management; understanding and setting up the optimum conditions for your own learning, e.g. to work with a particular friend, to do homework in a particular room.

6

7

STUDY SKILLS

1 Using a glossary.

2 Using a monolingual/bilingual dictionary.

3 Using reference books, relevant sections of the textbook, e.g. grammar summaries.

4 Using memorisation strategies.

5 Note-taking.

6 Planning revision; creating a timetable for what to revise and when.

7 Organising exercise book, notes, etc to facilitate revision and looking back for grammar points, vocabulary previously learned.

8 Working with friends, e.g. to test each other, check each other's work.

9

10

3   Why teach learning strategies?

Some learning strategies are described in the National Curriculum Programme of Study Part 1. They range from what could be described as basic study skills like using a dictionary or acquiring 'strategies for committing familiar language to memory', to more complex skills like the ability to 'use context and other clues to interpret meaning' or to 'redraft their writing to improve its accuracy'. Unsurprisingly, similar types of strategy are also identified in research exploring the teaching of English to non-native speakers (Oxford, 1990; Wenden, 1991). Even at university level, these strategies continue to be an important element of the language learning process. Whatever the language or the level, the point is that we cannot assume that learners will acquire strategies automatically.

The evidence is complex, but there seems to be some suggestion from recent research (O'Malley and Chamot, 1990) that some strategies may be easier than others and hence acquired earlier. These are the strategies used by low attainers and tend to be at a fairly simple level. It appears that these learners fail to move on to develop the more complex strategies used by the more successful language learners. Effective learners in both the reading and listening skill areas, for example, seem to use both a 'top-down' and a 'bottom-up' approach. In other words, they know how to identify the general gist of the text, to attack it at a global level, as well as how to perform word for word literal translation and analysis where necessary. Low attainers, on the other hand, seem to be limited to the 'bottom-up' approach to comprehension. Not only is their range narrower but they also seem to use strategies less frequently and to have problems in knowing which strategies to use when. Johnstone (1993) in his study of Scottish primary school pupils learning modern languages notes that, whereas the class as a whole may identify fourteen to fifteen strategies, each individual pupil may only be using two or three. The question then arises as to whether the teacher should simply accept pupils' limitations as inevitable or whether to intervene and set about teaching them the strategies they are lacking.

The importance of making explicit how to learn is particularly relevant, given the current concern about the underachievement of boys. This is a highly complex area that goes well beyond the confines of the modern language classroom, and it is not within the scope of this Pathfinder to discuss the issues. However, at the risk of stereotyping, if we try to identify some of the typical features that describe this particular group of underachieving boys, we may come up with a list that includes problems like:

- poor organisational skills;
- lack of forward planning;
- unwilling/unclear about how to revise;
- unwilling/ unclear about how to memorise vocabulary set for learning homework;
- unwilling/ unclear about how to check their work;
- tendency to make 'wild guesses' when reading rather than to think things through.

I have described the boys as 'unwilling/unclear' because it may not be as simple as a lack of motivation. For whatever reason, it may be that some boys lack a clear grasp of how to go about their learning and so enter a vicious circle whereby they feel that it is not even worth trying and therefore make even less progress. Rees and Graham (1995) suggest that:

> *If pupils are helped to perceive a link between the strategies employed and the resulting outcomes, however, their sense of control over their own learning could be heightened and a powerful source of motivation harnessed.*

Similarly the recent OFSTED report, *Boys and English,* states that;

> *Boys' performance improved when they had a clear understanding of the progress they needed in order to achieve well.*

The value of a cross-curricular approach to teaching strategies is evident. Collaboration across subjects could, for example, enable pupils to develop;

- dictionary skills, relevant to English as well as modern languages;
- study skills in lessons such as PSE;
- memorisation skills such as look-cover-test-check which apply to any subject area;
- strategies for reading for gist which may enable pupils to tackle the dense and complex texts they sometimes encounter in history, science or geography;
- drafting and redrafting strategies using Information Technology.

Over and above developing such specific skills, offering pupils insights into the learning process and how best they as individuals learn allows them to take a more equal role in their own education and to develop as confident, independent learners. It can equip them with tools that they will be able to use long after they leave school.

CiLT

4 How to teach learning strategies: the strategy training cycle

In reaching decisions as to which strategies to teach to which classes, it is clearly important to consider those that are most within pupils' reach. Monitoring and correcting sponaneous speech, for example, demands a higher level of linguistic competence than, say, memorisation strategies. The material in Chapter 2 may serve as a useful checklist or starting point in drawing up a list of the most appropriate strategies to teach a particular class.

Whichever type of strategy selected, the most important principle is to go about it systematically. Strategy training cannot be undertaken in a 'one-off' lesson or covered only in PSE periods. Pupils need to apply the strategies directly to modern languages tasks and to practise them extensively. Most writers on strategy training suggest a sequence of similar steps or stages. The next section gives some detailed examples of what these stages look like in the teaching of memorisation strategies, of reading strategies and of strategies for checking work. It might be useful to summarise the stages briefly first so that the principles behind each one are clear. It is interesting to note that steps 2, 4 and 5 are very similar to the cycle of presentation, practice and production used to teach the language of a new topic.

THE STRATEGY TRAINING CYCLE

1 AWARENESS RAISING

Pupils are set a task 'cold' ('learn these ten words for homework' for example) and then in the next lesson are asked how they went about it. They brainstorm the strategies they used and the ideas are collected on the board. The teacher explains that the aim now is to widen their repertoire of strategies. At this point, it is vital to persuade the class of the value of trying out new strategies. High attainers may need to be reminded not to become complacent and that, although they are making progress, they might improve even further (or simply find the work easier) if they adopt new strategies. Low attainers may need convincing that the problems they have experienced so far with learning the language may be due to lack of strategies, rather than lack of ability.

2 MODELLING

The teacher models each of the new strategies, making it clear exactly how to go about them. Sometimes the pupils themselves make excellent teachers, explaining to the rest of the class the strategies that work for them.

3 ACTION PLANNING/GOAL SETTING

Pupils are then ready to draw up their action plan, picking out the strategies that may be most useful for them to try. They may need some help in this. As teachers, we may know that if the problem is remembering how to pronounce the words properly for example, writing them out over and over again is unlikely to improve the situation. Pupils however do not always make the link between their own particular difficulty and the strategy that is likely to help them overcome it. They should also think through how they will monitor their own progress, how they will know that they have improved. It might even be useful to encourage them to fill out the action plan below. In this way, pupils can move towards taking responsibility for their learning but are provided with clear guidelines for doing so.

ACTION PLAN

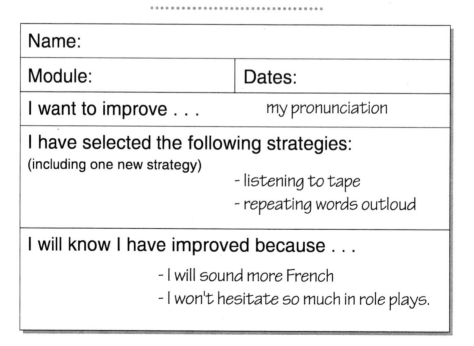

Name:	
Module:	Dates:
I want to improve . . .	my pronunciation

I have selected the following strategies:
(including one new strategy)

      - listening to tape
      - repeating words outloud

I will know I have improved because . . .

      - I will sound more French
      - I won't hesitate so much in role plays.

CiLT

4 EXTENSIVE PRACTICE

In all learning it is not enough to be told to do something and shown how. Learning to drive a car or to swim is not simply a matter of following instructions carefully. So, when we teach any topic, we devise a wide range of activities to practise the new language. Strategy training is no different and pupils will need a great deal of practice before they can use the strategies effectively. One way of supporting the practice stage is to provide a checklist of the new strategies discussed similar to those on pp17 and 21. In subsequent lessons pupils are reminded to tick any new strategies they have tried out and comment on them. They can then return to their action plan to see if the anticipated progress has or has not been made. If it has, they can move on to trying out some further strategies. If it has not, then teacher and pupil need to discuss their approach to using the strategies and to pinpoint what is going wrong.

5 FADING OUT THE REMINDERS

At some point, it is necessary to establish if these new strategies have been assimilated so that pupils automatically know when and how to use them. Setting a number of different tasks and discussing with pupils afterwards which strategies they used for each task can provide useful information as to whether further practice is needed.

The extent to which the discussions implicit in the cycle can be carried out in the target language will be discussed in the next sections, which explores the training cycle in action.

5   The strategy training cycle in action

The practical examples in this section are drawn from the work of the teachers and advisory teachers studying for the MA module on 'Developing Pupil Independence and Teaching Learner Strategies' run by CILT and Goldsmiths College.

They move from 'basic' strategies like memorisation to the more complex processes involved in checking and redrafting work.

TEACHING MEMORISATION STRATEGIES

I have often sat up preparing my lesson plan and materials and then realised at the last minute that it is 'Homework Night' and resorted to the well-tried teaching strategy of telling the pupils simply to 'learn the new words'. But do they know how to go about this? We frequently encounter pupils, even at 'A' level, who think that copying down lists of vocabulary or grammar rules will somehow ensure that they pass, by osmosis, into their heads. Pamela Dewey, Angelina Adams and Marian Carty followed the cycle of strategy training to help their pupils become more effective in this area. They started with 'Awareness raising'; setting pupils a learning homework as usual, the new vocabulary, for example, or a poem. In the next lesson they brainstormed with the pupils how they had gone about their homework and collected their ideas on the board. The teacher modelled some of the strategies, pupils others. It may not be obvious, for example, how to develop a 'photographic memory' or what is involved in 'mind maps'.

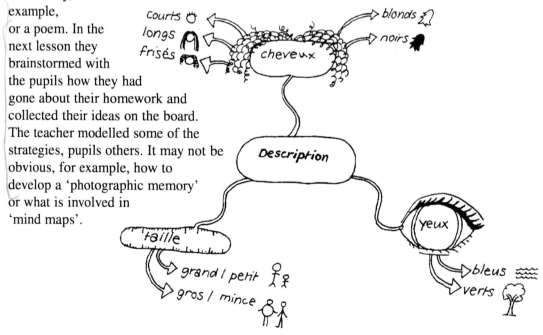

Pamela gives a good example of 'word association' from a pupil who remembered the word *montre* because 'it shows the time'. In terms of 'visual association', another pupil thought of keys (*clés*) made of clay. I remember the Swahili word for giraffe (*twiga*) by thinking that the giraffe's legs look like twigs.

Action plans are then written and a checklist drawn up, like the one devised by Marian Carty. In any subsequent learning task, pupils are reminded to tick off the strategies on their list to ensure that they are practising them. If they claim to have completed an oral pair work task, they can be asked which words they found the hardest to remember and to try out a new strategy to learn them.

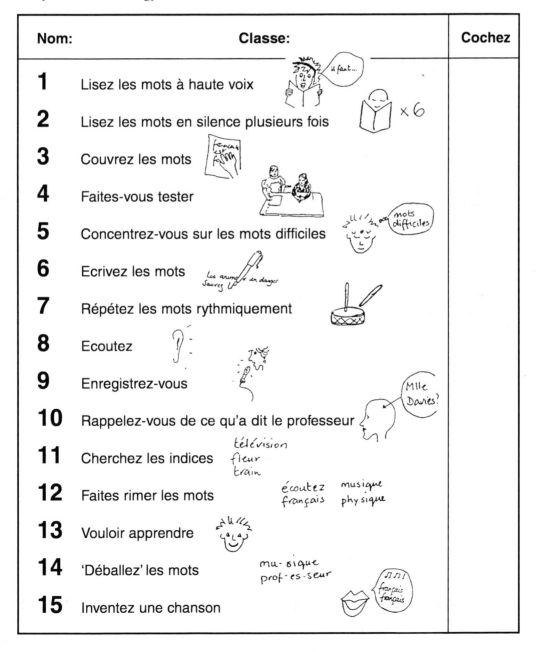

Nom:	Classe:	Cochez
1 Lisez les mots à haute voix		
2 Lisez les mots en silence plusieurs fois		
3 Couvrez les mots		
4 Faites-vous tester		
5 Concentrez-vous sur les mots difficiles		
6 Ecrivez les mots		
7 Répétez les mots rythmiquement		
8 Ecoutez		
9 Enregistrez-vous		
10 Rappelez-vous de ce qu'a dit le professeur		
11 Cherchez les indices		
12 Faites rimer les mots		
13 Vouloir apprendre		
14 'Déballez' les mots		
15 Inventez une chanson		

To increase pupils' motivation, Pamela produced bar charts plotting their results over a number of vocabulary tests.

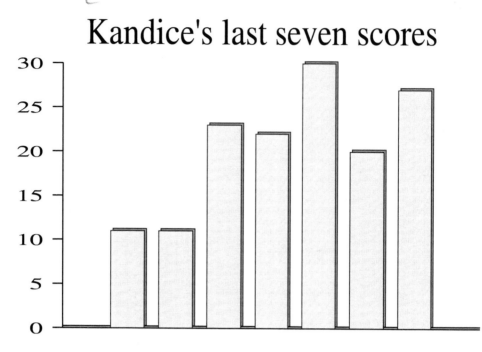

Kandice's last seven scores

TEACHING READING STRATEGIES

Fiona Lunsky wanted her Year 7 pupils to start to read for pleasure, but she was aware that many of them lacked the basic tools to cope on their own. So she started by brainstorming with them the strategies they were already using when they embarked on a text. She then selected the strategies she wanted to teach, based on those most likely to be within the grasp of the particular age range. Identifying cognates is relatively straightforward, for example, but strategies involving knowledge of the grammar of the language to work out the meaning may be more complex.

She went on to model the new strategies using the Dutch poem presented at the beginning of the book. This was followed up by a series of tasks where pupils practised the new strategies. Initial tasks may make the use of strategies very explicit:

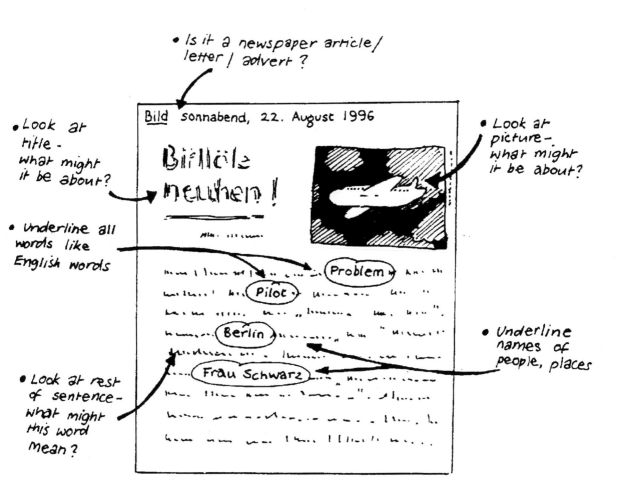

• Is it a newspaper article/ letter / advert ?

• Look at title - what might it be about?

• Underline all words like English words

• Look at rest of sentence - what might this word mean?

Bild sonnabend, 22. August 1996

Billige neuthen !

Problem
Pilot
Berlin
Frau Schwarz

• Look at picture - what might it be about?

• Underline names of people, places

In subsequent reading tasks, pupils can be reminded of the strategies by filling in the kind of chart, adapted from the Pathfinder *Reading for pleasure in a foreign language*.

LEARNING WORDS THROUGH READING

German	Looks like English	Guessed	Used word list	Carried on reading	Picture helped	Asked another student	Used dictionary	English
Teufelstich		✓						Boat
Birgit		✓						Bright
machen		✓						Match
Strandbad		✓						Sand

It is interesting to note that the pupil here only used the one strategy of 'guessing' and consistently guessed incorrectly. He appears to use 'wild card guessing', writing down the first thing that comes into his head. It might be that if he were encouraged to try out some of the other strategies on the list first, his guesses would become more accurate.

Two Goldsmiths PGCE students, Julie Chad and Sangeeta Chauhan, gave pupils the checklist opposite as a reminder.

Finally, pupils can return to their action plan, commenting not only on any improvement in their reading performance but hopefully also noting if their confidence in tackling new texts has increased, and perhaps even their enjoyment.

CiLT

VORSPRUNG DURCH LESENTECHNIK: CHECKLISTE

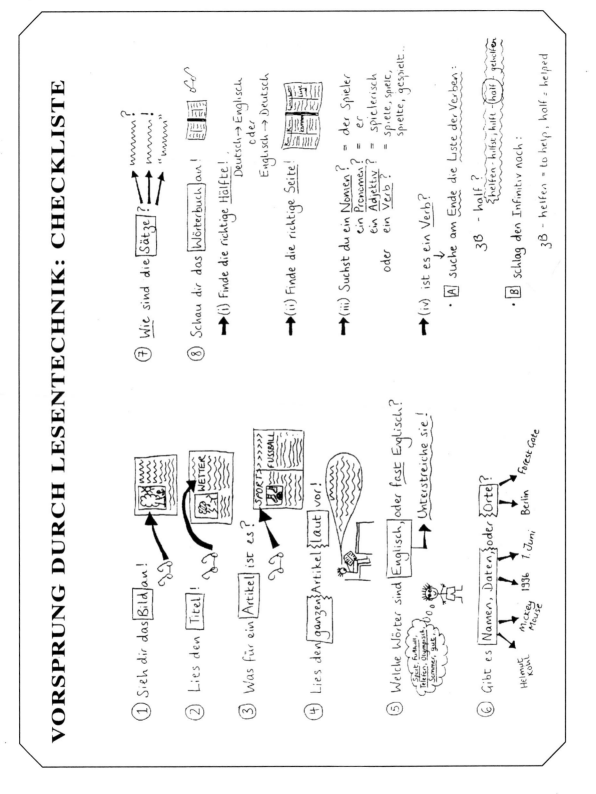

① Sieh dir das Bild an!

② Lies den Titel!

③ Was für ein Artikel ist es?

④ Lies den ganzen Artikel {laut} vor!

⑤ Welche Wörter sind Englisch, oder fast Englisch? Unterstreiche sie!

Sport, Fußball, Triathlon, Olympisch, Sommer, gut, ...

⑥ Gibt es Namen, Daten, oder Orte?

Helmut Kohl   Mickey Mouse   1936   7. Juni   Berlin   Forest Gate

⑦ Wie sind die Sätze? mmmm? mmmm! "mmmm"

⑧ Schau dir das Wörterbuch an!

→(i) Finde die richtige Hälfte!
  Deutsch → Englisch
  oder
  Englisch → Deutsch

→(ii) Finde die richtige Seite!

→(iii) Suchst du ein Nomen? = der Spieler
  ein Pronomen? = er
  ein Adjektiv? = spielerisch
  oder ein Verb? = spiele, spielt, spielte, spielte, gespielt...

→(iv) ist es ein Verb?

· Ⓐ suche am Ende die Liste der Verben:
  3B - half?
  helfen - hilfst, hilft -(half)- geholfen

· Ⓑ schlag den Infinitiv nach:
  3B - helfen = to help, half = helped

TEACHING PUPILS TO CHECK THEIR WORK

We often respond to the cry 'I've finished Miss' with 'Well, read it over again and correct any mistakes'. The completed work is handed in but it is not unusual to encounter frequent errors in gender, tense and word order. I have to confess to feeling often immensely frustrated when my own children have asked me to help them with their homework. I remind them to check it first before they show it to me. They assure me they have, but if I point to a particular word, they happily comment 'Oh, yes, it needs another *e*.' Frustrating though this is, it is perhaps understandable why pupils find checking their work so difficult, if we reflect on the processes involved. As successful learners, we probably use most if not all of the strategies identified in Chapter 2.

STRATEGIES FOR CHECKING WRITTEN WORK

'Self-evaluation: checking the outcomes of one's own language performance against an internal measure of completeness and accuracy'

May involve:

1 Sense monitoring: checking for meaning
2 Auditory monitoring: using one's ear for the language to make decisions
3 Visual monitoring: using one's eye for the language to make decisions
4 Style monitoring
5 Problem identification: identifying what you are unsure about
6 Resourcing: looking things up

Adapted from O'Malley and Chamot, *Learning strategies in second language acquisition* (Cambridge University Press, 1990)

It is possible that many of our pupils are not aware that we mean them to do all these things when we tell them to check their work, to take responsibility for spotting their errors for themselves. In line with the cycle of strategy training, we could start by discussing with them what they understand by checking their work and by modelling any unfamiliar strategies. To demonstrate how to check for meaning, for example, they could spot the mistakes in a simple text:

CiLT

Ich heiße Ute. Ich wohne in Berlin in einem Zweifamilienhaus. Ich bin Einzelkind, aber ich habe einen Hund und eine Katze. Ich bin sehr sportlich. Ich spiele nicht gern Fußball und Tennis. Sport ist langweilig. Ich habe zwei Brüder.

Although there is always a danger in presenting them with the wrong spellings, for the purpose of modelling 'visual monitoring', it might be legitimate to ask them to ring the correct word:

Schwimbad	*Schwimmbad*
geradaus	*geradeaus*
campagne	*campange*
mansion	*maison*

In terms of 'auditory monitoring', we can ask them to fill in a simple grid, listening to see if the adjective occurs before or after the noun, in phrases such as *un petit chat, un chat noir, une grande maison* and *une maison blanche*. They can then be given lists of further nouns and asked to create phrases with the adjectives on the basis of whether it 'sounds right'.

To remind them to use the strategies, we could ask them to fill in the form below each time they hand in written work. Items 4 and 5 could be altered according to the particular grammar point focussed on at any point in time. Insisting that they record at least one point that they looked up should develop the habit of using the dictionary and other reference books. Asking them at the end to identify what it is that they feel may still be wrong, inspite of the careful checking, serves a number of purposes. While the onus for 'getting it right' has been placed so far on the pupil, it is also important to acknowledge a legitimate role for the teacher, one where pupil and teacher can work together to overcome specific problems, and a dialogue can be entered into, albeit it in a written form. The pupil's comments may also provide the teacher with some insight into areas of confusion that are either specific to that learner or may be shared by other members of the class.

CHECKING MY WRITTEN WORK

STRATEGY	MISTAKE SPOTTED
1 Does it make sense?	
2 Does it sound right?	
3 Does it look right?	
4 Checking for tense	
5 Checking for gender	
6 Looked up	

What I am still unsure of:

Here, as in the examples of teaching memorisation and reading strategies, the aim is not only to put the responsibility onto pupils for their own learning but to provide them with a clear framework for how to go about it. A similarly structured approach to the teaching of collaborative skills can be found in the Pathfinder *Fair enough* (Harris, 1992) and to the teaching of dictionary skills in *Making effective use of the dictionary* (Berwick and Horsfall, 1996)

The question that inevitably arises is how to fit the systematic teaching of the different strategies into an already overcrowded timetable.

CiLT

6   There's no time!

BUILDING THE CYCLE INTO THE SCHEME OF WORK

If strategy training is to be integrated into the scheme of work, choices must be made about which strategies to teach when. Do we teach memorisation strategies to Year 7, then reading strategies when they reach Year 8 and checking work at Year 9? Or do we select some reading strategies as appropriate for Year 7, others for Year 9 and so on? The second option seems the more sensible, but it does involve some serious planning to ensure progression over Key Stages 3 and 4.

At first sight, strategy training looks extremely time-consuming, and there may be concerns about how to make the space to include it in the scheme of work. It is worth exploring just how much extra time may be involved, by taking a practical example of teaching pupils strategies for memorising grammar rules. Grammar is currently the source of considerable debate. There seems to be a growing consensus, however, that at some point, once the pupils have been exposed to the language within a communicative context and have practised it, they should be asked to deduce the rules and encouraged to learn them. Some suggestions for the strategies they could use to remember the rules are given on p26; others could be added under items 8 and 9. Unsurprisingly, many of the strategies are similar to those involved in memorising words;

The sequence of lessons on p27 sets out what might be involved in training a class of Year 7 or 8 pupils to use some of the strategies and broadly how much time it would take. Most modern language teachers have their own preferred way of teaching the topic 'Hobbies'. They might, however, share the view that by the end of it, at least the high attainers should have some understanding that the gender of a hobby can alter *aller à la* to *au* and *faire de la* to *du*.

The first few lessons focus on teaching the new vocabulary and perhaps asking the pupils to spot the rule for hobbies used with *aller* and to learn it for homework. Lesson 3 is the only lesson in the sequence entirely devoted to strategy training. Pupils brainstorm how they went about their learning homework, model new strategies and devise their action plan. Lesson 4 proceeds as it usually would. Lesson 5 might require five to ten minutes to return comments on action plans, but this could be done while pupils were working on their creative outcomes. Lesson 10, like Lesson 5, may require more time as pupils discuss their progress. However, it may be time well spent since once these strategies have been assimilated, there will hopefully be 'spin-offs' in terms of more effective learning of subsequent grammar rules.

	Memorisation strategy	Activity
1	Representing sounds in memory	• Sing rules to tune/rap, e.g. *je regarde, tu regardes,* etc to tune of 'Happy Birthday' (cf *With a song in my scheme of work* by Steven Fawkes, CILT, 1995).
2	Using physical response	• Thinking of hot/cold for gender; writing feminine nouns in yellow, masculine in green. • *Ich habe mein Buch* **vergessen;** knocking table to mark verb at end of sentence.
3	Using mechanical techniques	• Sorting words into piles, e.g. verbs with *sein* and those with *haben.*
4	Using memory strategies for retrieval	• Acronyms, e.g. for verbs with *être* and *avoir.*
5	Using imagery	• Drawings, e.g. *à la disco, patinoire, piscine.*
6	Semantic mapping	• Topic webs.
7	Be on the lookout	• Underline all examples of rule in a text. • Gap-fill and return to next day.
8		
9		

Adapted from Oxford R, *Language learning strategies* (Heinle and Heinle, 1990)

CiLT

LESSON	ACTIVITIES	STAGE OF CYCLE
Lessons 1/2	Teach new vocab: *aimer + aller à la/au*. Pupils deduce rule for *aller à la/au*. Class survey. Homework; pupils learn rules.	
Lesson 3	Brainstorm: how did they learn the rules? What do they find hard about learning grammar rules? Discuss some new ways of learning and illustrate. Groups make up a song, picture, etc. Discuss how they will know if getting better at learning rules: don't have to look rules up all the time/don't just put any old thing down/know what to look for when checking work/fewer mistakes/more fun. Homework: write out action plan and two new activities they will try in future.	Awareness-raising. Modelling. Goal setting.
Lesson 4	Give out checklist of ways of learning, including their own suggestions. Teach: *faire du/ de la/des*. Pupils deduce rule for *du/de la/des*. Pupils look up four new *faire* activities in dictionary and decide if *faire du* or *de la*. Homework: use two strategies to learn the rule.	Explicit reminders. Trying out new possibilities.
Lessons 5/6	Return action plans with any comments. Consolidation of hobbies and creative outcomes.	
Lessons 7/8	New topic. New rules. Model some new strategies.	
Lessons 10/11	Homework: review goals. How are they now finding learning grammar rules? Have their goals been achieved? Set new goals: consolidate existing strategies/try out new ones.	Monitoring learning and progress.

WHAT ABOUT THE TARGET LANGUAGE?

How much of the cycle could be taught in the target language? We have seen on p17 that the checklists can be written in the target language, provided they are accompanied by visual support. Perhaps even the action plan could be in the target language, if pupils were given a list of possible expressions from which to choose. With most pre-sixth form classes, however, it is likely that the discussions in Lessons 3 and 10 would have to be in English initially. The aim here is to get all pupils participating and reflecting on their learning. The effort of explaining themselves in the target language may well deter all but the highest attainers from contributing to the discussion. In the long term, any disadvantages produced by not using the target language one hundred per cent of the time may be offset by an improvement in pupil motivation, independence and performance. As pupils begin to become familiar with the process of reflecting on their own learning, however, they can be taught gradually how to make their comments in the target language and key expressions can be displayed around the classroom. Explaining that *je trouve ça difficile* applies equally well to difficulties encountered in memorising vocabulary, as it does to different school subjects, with the added bonus that how they approach their language learning may well be of more immediate concern than whether they do or do not like geography, maths, etc. As David Little (1993) points out:

> *The learner's acceptance of responsibility for his or her learning entails the gradual development of a capacity for independent and flexible use of the target language. Thus all autonomy projects will necessarily tend to create the circumstances in which learners are engaged in activities that require them to use the target language for genuinely communicative purposes.*

Issues such as time and target language cannot be easily resolved. Answers will vary according to the class taught, to the school situation and departmental priorities. They can, however, be discussed in departmental meetings and in the last section, we make some suggestions for moving forward.

7   Taking it further

If we want pupils to reflect on their own learning and to take greater responsibility for making progress, what are the implications for us as their teachers? Could we also undertake a similar process but in relation to our teaching? It is interesting to note that the cycle of strategy training is very similar to the cycle of action-based research, which allows teachers to evaluate systematically new initiatives they try out with their classes. Just as the pupils start the cycle by taking stock of their own strengths and weaknesses, we may begin by identifying the problems of a particular class, and how we currently approach teaching them. What is the immediate area of concern with these pupils and which strategies could be taught to address it? Clear goals are then established and an action plan devised. How are we going to teach those strategies and over what period of time? How are we going to know if we have been successful? Having implemented the plan, we can then monitor any progress made to date, pinpointing remaining difficulties or further questions and identifying ways forward. Often the very process of tackling a problem head-on throws up new issues and so the cycle starts again, both for us and our pupils.

Hence, in terms of strategy training, the following process might be useful:

1 Start by identifying the most pressing concern; whether it is the need to encourage more extensive reading, or to ensure that Year 11 pupils check their work more carefully.

2 Identify which strategies would be relevant for addressing the problem. Here it may be helpful to use the checklists in Chapter 2 as a starting point but, since they are mostly drawn from research focussed on advanced learners, it may be necessary to add to them by:

- observing which strategies high attainers in the class are already using to tackle that skill area successfully;
- observing which strategies appear to be lacking among the low attainers in the class;
- observing successful strategies used by any older pupils in Year 11 or the sixth form that could be passed on to the class in question;
- reflecting on our own use of strategies. What was it that helped us to become successful linguists?

Especially with younger learners it may also be necessary to 'unpack' some strategies even further. For example, the reading strategy of 'Going for gist, skipping inessential words' may involve:

- skimming to spot familar words;
- initially approximating new words or parts of words to a rough meaning; 'there remains' for *restaient,* for example;
- initially leaving out some of the minor words not essential to the overall meaning of the sentence, e.g. translating *Davon kaufe ich mir meist Kleidung. Die muß ich nämlich selbst zahlen* as 'I buy most of my clothes. I have to pay for them myself'.

3 Liaise with English, PSE, and SEN colleagues to find out what strategies they already teach and how.

4 Select those strategies that seem to be most useful for that particular class or age group and even decide which ones to teach first. Two PGCE students, Cheryl Michael and Heather Wright, for example, found that by teaching pupils to recognise cognates first, they gained their trust and their interest and were able to go on to more complex strategies.

5 Build the cycle into the scheme of work, deciding when to start it, how to integrate it into subsequent lessons, etc.

6 Make any necessary materials; a checklist, poster or other ways of reminding pupils.

7 Monitor if the strategy training appears to justify the time taken and the use of English. Is there any long-term improvement in the problem area identified? Have all pupils benefitted from the strategy training or only a limited number? Who has failed to try out new strategies? Why? What do the pupils think of it themselves?

8 Decide on ways of 'tightening up' the training to involve more of the pupils or of increasing the use of the target language.

The reality is that experimenting with a new teaching approach can be time-consuming and even daunting, so it is often easiest to iron out any 'teething problems' with a fairly amenable class! But if we are prepared to take the risk of trying out the strategy training cycle, it may not only enable the pupils to take greater responsibility for their progress and discover more about how they learn, we may also come to a greater understanding of the learning process ourselves.

As Leni Dam (1990), a pioneer in the movement towards greater pupil autonomy, pointed out:

The pivot of the whole learning/teaching process is without doubt the recurring evaluation, a constant focus for both teacher and learner on:

What am I doing?
Why am I doing it?
How am I doing it?
What can it be used for?

> Translation of the poem on p1:
>
> *An apple is red,*
> *The sun is yellow,*
> *The sky is blue,*
> *A leaf is green,*
> *A cloud is white . . .*
> *And the earth is brown.*
> *And would you now be able*
> *to answer the question:*
> *What colour is love?*

The illustration and poem featured on p1 of this Pathfinder have been taken from *Welke kleur de liefde?* by Joan Walsh Anglund, published by Zomer & Keuning, Wageningen, Holland.

References

For a detailed picture of the literature underlying the summary in Chapter 2, readers might initially refer to the following writers:

McDonough S H, *Strategy and skill in learning a foreign language* (London: Edward Arnold, 1995)

O'Malley J M and A U Chamot, *Learning strategies in second language acquisition* (Cambridge: Cambridge University Press, 1990)

Oxford R L, *Language learning strategies* (Boston: Heinle and Heinle, 1990)

Other books referred to are:

Berwick G and P Horsfall, *Making effective use of the dictionary* (London: CILT, 1996)

Bialystok E, *Communication strategies: a psychological analysis of second language use* (Oxford: Basil Blackwell, 1990)

Dam L, 'Learner autonomy in practice' in Gathercole G (ed), *Autonomy in language learning* (London: CILT, 1990)

Dickinson L, *Self-instruction in language learning* (Cambridge: Cambridge University Press, 1987)

Harris V, *Fair enough? Equal opportunities and modern languages* (London: CILT, 1992)

Holec H (ed), *Autonomy and self-directed learning: present fields of application* (Strasbourg: Council of Europe, 1988)

Graham S and F Rees, 'Gender differences in language learning; the question of control' in *Language Learning Journal*, 11: 18–19 (1995)

Grenfell M and V Harris, 'How do pupils learn (Part 1)' in *Language Learning Journal*, 8: 22–25 (1993)

Johnstone R, L Low, J Duffield and S Brown, *Evaluating foreign languages in primary schools* (Stirling: SCILT, 1993)

CiLT

Little D, *Learner autonomy 1: definitions, issues and problems* (Dublin: Authentik, 1991)

Little D, 'Learning as dialogue: the dependence of learner autonomy on teacher autonomy'. Symposium on Learner Autonomy at AILA 93: Amsterdam (1993)

Little D, 'Strategies in language learning and teaching: some introductory reflections'. Paper given at CILT Research Forum: Strategies in foreign language learning (London, 16 May 1997)

Nunan D, 'Closing the gap between learning and instruction' in *TESOL Quarterly,* 29: 133–158

Page B (ed), *Letting go — taking hold* (London: CILT, 1992)

Swarbrick A, *Reading for pleasure in a foreign language* (London: CILT, 1990)

Wenden A, *Learner strategies for learner autonomy* (Cambridge: Prentice Hall, 1991)